tapas

tapas

RYLAND
PETERS
& SMALL
LONDON NEW YORK

First published in the United Kingdom in 2007
by Ryland Peters & Small
20–21 Jockey's Fields
London WC1R 4BW
www.rylandpeters.com

10 9 8 7 6 5

ISBN: 978-1-84597-394-0

A CIP record for this book is available from the
British Library.

Printed and bound in China

Designer Jo Fernandes
Editor Rachel Lawrence
Picture Research Emily Westlake
Production Sheila Smith
Art Director Anne-Marie Bulat
Publishing Director Alison Starling

Notes

All spoon measurements are level unless
otherwise stated.
Barbecues, ovens and grills should be heated
to the required temperature before adding
the food.
Eggs are large unless otherwise specified.
Uncooked or partially cooked eggs should not
be served to the very old, frail, young children,
pregnant women or those with compromised
immune systems.
Specialist Spanish ingredients are available in
larger supermarkets, Spanish and sometimes
Italian delicatessens.

contents

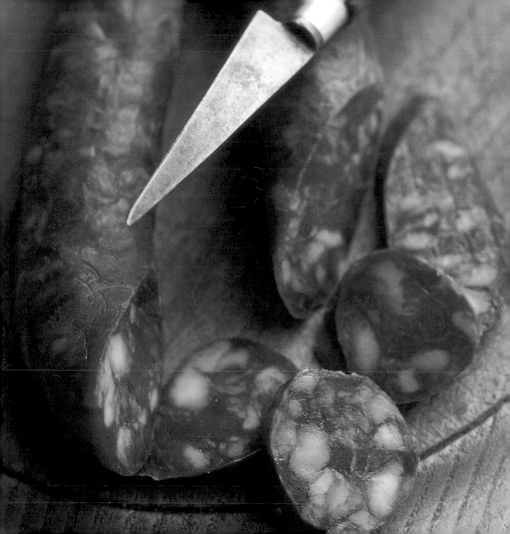

a taste sensation

One of the defining features of Spanish food culture, tapas bars, or *tascas*, are found all over Spain. Before lunch or dinner, they are crowded with people catching up over a glass of sherry, wine or beer accompanied by little savoury snacks. From little bowls of marinated olives or chunks of Manchego cheese to deep-fried seafood, these delicious dishes are the ultimate in bar food.

The word *tapa* means lid and, while the subject of much debate, it is thought that this originally referred to a piece of bread placed on top of a glass of sherry to keep flies away. This was often served with a slice of cheese or ham and so the tradition began. Today the range of tapas dishes is astounding and reflects the diversity of ingredients in Spain, which include exquisite cured meats, seafood and cheese, as well as delicate flavourings such as oak-smoked paprika and saffron.

While tapas is traditionally a pre-lunch or pre-dinner snack, it can be a meal in itself. The tapas crawl, or *tapeo*, is a long-standing tradition in many towns and cities, with customers moving from one bar to the next and sampling each one's specialities as they go.

Tapas is a wonderfully sociable way to eat and re-creating these irresistible dishes at home is a lot of fun. Many of them can be prepared in advance and served at a leisurely pace over several hours. So why not invite a few friends around, crack open a bottle of Rioja and feast upon this sensational fingerfood.

fish and seafood

albóndigas de bacalao
cod balls

Put the cod in a bowl, cover with cold water and keep in the refrigerator for at least 24 hours. Change the water occasionally.

Prick the potatoes with a skewer, then bake in a preheated oven at 200°C (400°F) Gas 6 for 1 hour or until soft on the inside. Scoop the flesh out of the skins into a bowl and mash.

Put the cod in a saucepan, cover with cold water, add the bay leaf, bring to the boil and simmer for 30 minutes. Let cool, then remove the skin and flake the flesh into a bowl, making sure to remove all the bones. Add to the mashed potatoes, then stir in the garlic, parsley, pepper and 2 tablespoons of the cod cooking liquid. Roll the mixture into walnut-sized balls. Put in a bowl, cover with clingfilm and chill in the refrigerator for 2–3 hours.

Put the egg in a bowl, add 1 tablespoon water and beat lightly. Dip the cod balls in the egg, then roll in flour on a plate. Fill a deep frying pan or an electric deep-fryer one-third with oil, or to the manufacturer's recommended level. Heat to 195°C (380°F) or until a 1-cm cube of bread browns in 30 seconds. Cook the balls, in batches, for about 3 minutes or until golden brown. Remove with a slotted spoon and drain on crumpled kitchen paper. Serve hot with alioli.

125 g salt cod

300 g potatoes

1 bay leaf

1 garlic clove, crushed

1 tablespoon freshly chopped flat leaf parsley

freshly ground white pepper

1 egg

plain flour

oil, for frying

alioli (page 58) or lemon wedges, to serve

an electric deep-fryer (optional)

serves 4

gambas al ajillo
garlic prawns

48 small uncooked prawns, about 600 g, shelled and deveined, with tail shell left on

4 tablespoons extra virgin olive oil

8 garlic cloves, bruised

6 small dried chillies

8 small fresh bay leaves

juice of ½ lemon

sea salt

alioli (page 58), to serve

4 individual cazuelas (terracotta ramekins) preheated in a hot oven

serves 4

To prepare the prawns, put them on a plate and sprinkle lightly with salt. Heat the olive oil in a frying pan, add the garlic and fry until brown. Add the chillies, bay leaves and prawns all at once and fry without turning until the prawns are crusted and curled on one side, then turn them over and crust the other side, about 3½ minutes in total.

Transfer to the preheated cazuelas, sprinkle with lemon juice and top with a spoonful of alioli, or serve a small bowl of alioli on the side. Serve immediately while still bubbling hot.

boquerones en vinagre
marinated anchovies

To clean the anchovies, run your finger down the belly side and open up the fish. Pull the spine from the head and separate it from the flesh. Remove the head. Wash the fish and let dry on kitchen paper.

Put the anchovies in a plastic container and pour in the vinegar. Let marinate in the refrigerator overnight. Rinse the anchovies and put in a serving dish with the garlic, parsley and olive oil. Cover and chill overnight in the refrigerator. Return to room temperature before serving with bread or as an accompaniment to another dish. You can return them to the refrigerator to eat another day – they only get better with time.

*Note If fresh anchovies are unavailable, use any small fish. Aim for 6–8 cm long.

150 g fresh anchovies*

100 ml good-quality white vinegar

3 garlic cloves, sliced

1 tablespoon chopped fresh flat leaf parsley

100 ml olive oil

serves 4

tigre tapas
mussels in overcoats

Tap the mussels gently against the work surface and discard any that don't close. Put the mussels, onion, bay leaves and stock in a large saucepan and cover. Bring to the boil and cook hard for 2–3 minutes or until the shells open, then remove the cooked mussels and discard any that haven't opened. Boil the cooking liquid for several minutes to intensify the flavour, then pour through a sieve. Reserve 125 ml of the cooking liquid.

Fill a deep frying pan or an electric deep-fryer one-third full with oil, or to the manufacturer's recommended level. Heat to 190°C (375°F) or until a 1-cm cube of bread browns in 30 seconds.

To make the batter, sift the flour, paprika and black pepper into a bowl. Grind the saffron threads finely with the salt using a mortar and pestle. Add to the dry ingredients. Put the egg whites in another bowl and whisk until soft peaks form, then set aside.

Add the reserved mussel liquid and egg yolks to the flour and whisk to make a soft batter. Fold in the egg whites.

Dip the mussels, still on their half-shells, into the batter. Add to the hot oil, in batches of 5–6. Cook for 2–2½ minutes or until golden, crisp and fragrant, then serve.

500 g large, live mussels, in the shell, scrubbed, rinsed and debearded

1 onion, sliced

2 fresh bay leaves, bruised

150 ml hot stock, white wine or fino sherry

extra virgin olive oil or peanut oil, for deep-frying

batter

100 g plain flour

1 teaspoon oak-smoked hot Spanish paprika (page 23)

½ teaspoon freshly ground black pepper

a pinch of saffron threads

½ teaspoon coarse sea salt

2 eggs, separated

an electric deep-fryer (optional)

serves 4

500 g small fresh clams

a pinch of saffron threads

1 tablespoon olive oil

½ small onion, finely chopped

2 garlic cloves, crushed

75 ml dry sherry

2 tablespoons tomato purée

1 tablespoon freshly chopped flat leaf parsley

a pinch of oak-smoked sweet Spanish paprika (page 23)

a pinch of cayenne

1 tablespoon ground almonds

bread, to serve

serves 4

almejas a la marinera
clams in tomato and saffron sauce

To clean the clams, put them in a bowl of cold salty water and let soak for 2 hours. This should help get rid of some of the grit. Put the saffron threads in a bowl with 1 tablespoon of hot water and let soak.

Heat the olive oil in a casserole dish over gentle heat, then add the onion and cook for 3 minutes. Add the garlic, sherry, tomato purée, parsley, paprika, cayenne, saffron with its juice and 50 ml water. Bring to the boil and boil for 4 minutes.

Add the clams, cover with a lid and cook for 4 minutes until the shells steam open (discard any that don't). Stir in the ground almonds and cook for 1 further minute. Remove from the heat and set aside, covered with a lid, for 5 minutes. Serve warm with plenty of bread to mop up the juices.

sepia con alioli
squid with mayonnaise

100–200 g semolina flour

½–1 teaspoon sea salt

½–1 teaspoon dried oregano
or marjoram leaves,
crumbled

8 medium squid or
cuttlefish tubes,
sliced into 1-cm rounds

extra virgin olive oil,
for deep-frying

alioli, to serve (page 58)

lemon halves, to serve

an electric deep-fryer
(optional)

serves 4

Put the semolina flour, salt and oregano in a bowl. Pat the squid or cuttlefish rings dry with kitchen paper and toss them in the flour mixture until well coated.

Fill a deep frying pan or an electric deep-fryer one-third full with oil, or to the manufacturer's recommended level. Heat to 190°C (375°F) or until a 1-cm cube of bread browns in 30 seconds. Fry the prepared squid or cuttlefish in the hot oil in batches of about 8. Cook for 30–45 seconds, the minimum time it takes to set the seafood to firm whiteness and make the coating crisp. Remove, drain and keep hot. Continue until all are cooked.

Serve a pile of squid rings on each plate, with ½ lemon, if using, and a large spoonful of alioli.

pulpo a la vinagreta
marinated octopus

If the octopus hasn't been frozen or tenderized by a fishmonger, you should throw it against a hard surface 10 times or more. Put it on a chopping board, cut off the head just below the eyes, then squeeze out and discard the beak, which is in the centre of the tentacles. You can discard the head part, or cut off above the eyes and rinse out the bodies.

Bring a large saucepan of water to the boil, then blanch the octopus for 30 seconds at a time, repeating 4–5 times. Return to the saucepan, cover with a lid and simmer for 1 hour.

Test the octopus for tenderness – if it's still tough, continue cooking for another 20 minutes. Remove from the heat, let cool, then drain. Cut the tentacles into 2-cm lengths and the bodies into bite-sized pieces.

Heat the olive oil in a frying pan, then add the vinegar, garlic, 2 tablespoons of the parsley, paprika, chilli flakes, capers and octopus. Bring to the boil, then simmer for 3 minutes. Transfer to a plastic or ceramic dish, let cool, season, then let marinate in the refrigerator overnight.

Serve at room temperature with lemon juice and parsley.

4 baby octopus, about 500 g

3 tablespoons fruity olive oil

2 tablespoons red wine vinegar

2 garlic cloves, crushed

3 tablespoons freshly chopped flat leaf parsley, plus extra to serve

½ teaspoon oak-smoked sweet Spanish paprika (page 23)

½ teaspoon dried chilli flakes

1 tablespoon capers, chopped

juice of 1 lemon

sea salt and freshly ground black pepper

serves 4

meat and poultry

cordero al limón
lamb with lemon

Cut the lamb into 2 cm cubes, put in a bowl, cover with the pineapple slices and let marinate overnight, covered, in the refrigerator.

Stick the cloves into the lemon half and put it in a roasting dish. Add the garlic, olive oil and rosemary. Remove the lamb from the pineapple and rub in the onion and paprika. Add the lamb to the roasting dish and cook in a preheated oven at 150°C (300°F) Gas 2 for 15 minutes. Remove the dish from the oven, cover with aluminium foil and set aside for 10 minutes. Serve warm.

*Note Spanish paprika is available in three forms: *pimentón dulce* is mild and sweet; *pimentón picante* is spicy hot; while *pimentón agridulce* is bittersweet. There are also smoked versions which are made from chillies hung whole in traditional mud houses above oak fires that burn for 10–15 days. All these varieties are available in large supermarkets or specialist food shops.

250 g lean lamb

225 g canned
pineapple slices

10 cloves

1 lemon, halved

5 garlic cloves

2 tablespoons olive oil

a sprig of rosemary

½ small onion,
finely chopped

a pinch of oak-smoked
sweet Spanish paprika*

serves 4

pinchitos morunos
spicy moorish kebabs

2 tablespoons olive oil

2 garlic cloves, crushed

1 dried red chilli, crushed

1 teaspoon ground cumin

1 teaspoon ground fennel

1 teaspoon oak-smoked sweet Spanish paprika (page 23)

juice of 1 lemon

2 tablespoons freshly chopped flat leaf parsley

1 tablespoon dry sherry

500 g lean pork fillet

metal kebab skewers, or bamboo, soaked in water for 30 minutes

serves 4

Put the oil, garlic, chilli, cumin, fennel, paprika, lemon juice, parsley and sherry in a bowl and mix well. Cut the pork into 2-cm cubes and add to the bowl. Cover and chill overnight in the refrigerator.

When ready to cook, preheat an overhead grill until very hot. Thread the pork onto the skewers and grill for 10 minutes, turning often – take care not to overcook the meat. Remove from the heat and set aside for 10 minutes. Serve warm.

150 g minced pork

150 g minced veal

1 teaspoon lemon juice

1 small onion, chopped

4 garlic cloves, crushed

2 tablespoons freshly chopped flat leaf parsley

½ teaspoon grated nutmeg

½ teaspoon ground cloves

30 g dried breadcrumbs

1 egg

1 tablespoon single cream

2 tablespoons olive oil

125 ml white wine

400 g canned chopped tomatoes

½ teaspoon oak-smoked sweet Spanish paprika (page 23)

1 fresh bay leaf

sea salt and freshly ground white pepper

plain flour, for dusting

serves 4

albóndigas
meat balls in tomato sauce

To make the meat balls, put the pork and veal in a bowl, then add the lemon juice, half of the chopped onion and crushed garlic, followed by the parsley, nutmeg, cloves, breadcrumbs, egg, cream, salt and pepper. Mix well, then roll into walnut-sized balls. Dust with flour.

Heat the olive oil in a casserole dish until smoking, then add the meat balls, and fry until browned on all sides. Reduce the heat to low. Add the wine, tomatoes, the remaining onion and garlic, with the paprika, bay leaf and 100 ml water. Cover and simmer for 1 hour. The mixture should be quite liquid, so add extra water if necessary. Serve warm.

Note These meat balls can be made in advance as they will reheat well.

chorizo al vino
chorizo in red wine

Cut the chorizo into 1-cm chunks. Heat half the olive oil in a large, non-stick frying pan until very hot. Add half the chorizo and fry on both sides for 1 minute each. Remove with a slotted spoon and keep hot. Add the remaining oil and remaining chorizo. Cook and remove as before.

Add the wine and thyme, if using, to the pan and swirl to dissolve the sediment. Cook gently to thicken and reduce the sauce. Pour the sauce over the hot chorizo, sprinkle with pepper and serve with chunks of torn bread for dipping.

Note Chorizo comes in many different varieties – you can get smoked, unsmoked, fresh and cured. A spicy chorizo works well in this recipe. If chorizo is difficult to find, use cooked, garlicky Polish pork sausage (kielbasa) and add 2 teaspoons of paprika to the juices in the pan.

750 g uncooked chorizo or other dense, garlic-flavoured pork sausage

2 tablespoons extra virgin olive oil

150 ml red wine

4 sprigs of thyme (optional)

freshly ground black pepper

torn bread, for dipping

serves 4

ensalada catalana de garbanzos
catalan chickpea salad

Heat the olive oil in a frying pan, add the onion, garlic, chorizo
and bay leaves and sauté over gentle heat for 5 minutes or until
softened but not browned. Stir in the pine nuts and chickpeas
with a little of their liquid. Heat through until the flavours are
combined, mashing a little with a fork.

Sprinkle with pepper and chopped tomato and serve hot, warm
or cool, but never chilled.

Note This recipe uses chorizo or sausage for ease, although
traditionally it would have been made with pieces of chopped
cooked pork, or sometimes *morcilla* (black pudding) or *butifarra*
(white sausage).

3 tablespoons extra virgin
olive oil

1 red onion, sliced

2 garlic cloves, chopped

200 g chorizo or other
dense garlic-flavoured pork
sausage, sliced

2 bay leaves, bruised

2 tablespoons pine nuts,
toasted in a dry frying pan

400 g canned chickpeas,
drained, with 2 tablespoons
of their liquid

coarsely ground
black pepper

1 small tomato,
finely chopped

serves 4

250 ml milk

½ small onion, sliced

1 bay leaf

2 peppercorns

a sprig of thyme

2 tablespoons unsalted butter, about 25 g

3 tablespoons plain flour

a pinch of oak-smoked sweet Spanish paprika (page 23)

a pinch of freshly grated nutmeg

150 g jamón serrano (Spanish ham), finely chopped

100 g cooked chicken breast, finely chopped

300 g dried breadcrumbs

2 eggs, lightly beaten

oil, for deep-frying

an electric deep-fryer (optional)

serves 4

croquetas de jamón
ham croquettes

Put the milk in a saucepan, add the onion, bay leaf, peppercorns and thyme and heat until just below boiling point. Remove from the heat, let cool, then strain into a bowl.

Put the butter in the saucepan, melt gently, stir in the flour and cook for 2 minutes, stirring constantly. When the roux begins to brown, slowly add the strained milk, stirring to prevent lumps forming. Continue to cook, stirring in the paprika and nutmeg.

Heat 1 tablespoon oil in a frying pan, add the ham and fry until the fat starts to run. Add the ham and chicken to the white sauce and cook until the sauce thickens, about 2 minutes. Remove from the heat and let cool. Refrigerate for 3 hours or overnight.

Shape the mixture into croquettes about 6 x 2 cm. Lightly roll in the breadcrumbs, dip in the beaten eggs and roll in the breadcrumbs again. Chill for 1 hour or overnight.

When ready to cook, fill a saucepan or deep-fryer one-third with oil, or to the manufacturer's recommended level. Heat to 195°C (380°F) or until a 1-cm cube of bread browns in 30 seconds. Fry the croquettes, in batches if necessary, for 3 minutes or until golden brown. Serve immediately.

pollo al ajillo
chicken with garlic

1 tablespoon sweet Spanish paprika (page 23)

1 tablespoon plain flour

1.75 kg chicken pieces, such as thighs and breasts (but no drumsticks)

100 ml extra virgin olive oil

15 garlic cloves, unpeeled but slightly bruised

1 fresh bay leaf

125 ml medium dry sherry

1 tablespoon coarsely chopped fresh flat leaf parsley, plus extra to serve

sea salt and freshly ground black pepper

a heat-diffusing mat

serves 4

Put the paprika, flour, salt and pepper in a plastic bag and shake to mix. Add the chicken pieces and toss again until the chicken is evenly coated. Leave in the bag for 30 minutes or longer.

Heat the olive oil in a frying pan, add the garlic and fry for 2 minutes, then remove with a slotted spoon. Add the chicken pieces (if necessary do half at a time, but remember to remove half the garlic-infused oil) and fry for 5 minutes. Add the fried garlic and continue frying for 5 minutes until the chicken is golden on all sides.

Add the bay leaf and sherry and bring to the boil. Lower the heat and simmer gently on a heat-diffusing mat for about 30 minutes until tender. (Breast pieces will cook faster, so remove them about 10 minutes before the end of cooking.) Pile onto a serving platter and sprinkle with parsley.

Note Although Pollo al Ajillo is traditionally cooked on top of the stove, it could be baked in a preheated oven at 190°C (375°F) Gas 5 for 35 minutes or until cooked through.

vegetables and little extras

gazpacho

Grind the garlic with a pinch of salt using a mortar and pestle.

Put the bread in a saucer with a little water and let soak. Put the ground garlic, bread, tomatoes, onion, cucumber and vinegar in a blender and purée until smooth. Keep the motor running and add the olive oil in a slow and steady stream. Add salt and pepper to taste, then add the sugar.

Pour the mixture through a sieve into a bowl, adding more seasoning and vinegar if necessary. Chill in the refrigerator overnight and serve in small bowls or glasses with a little chopped cucumber on top.

1 garlic clove

1 slice white bread, crusts removed

4 ripe juicy tomatoes, skinned and deseeded

1 tablespoon grated onion

¼ small cucumber, peeled and deseeded, plus extra to serve

1 tablespoon Spanish red wine vinegar

2 tablespoons olive oil

1 teaspoon sugar

sea salt and freshly ground black pepper

serves 4

tortilla española
spanish omelette

250 ml olive oil

4 potatoes, about 500 g,
cut into 1-cm cubes

1 onion, thinly sliced

6 eggs

4 tablespoons chopped
flat-leaf parsley (optional)

coarse sea salt and freshly
ground black pepper

a deep frying pan,
23 cm diameter

serves 4

Heat the olive oil in a frying pan until hot, add the potatoes and
onions, turn to coat with the oil, then reduce the temperature.
Cook for 15 minutes or until soft, turning often without letting
them brown. Remove the potatoes and onions with a slotted
spoon and drain on kitchen paper. Pour the oil into a small bowl.

Put the eggs, salt and pepper into a bowl and beat with a fork.
Add the potatoes and onions to the bowl, stir gently, then stir in
the parsley, if using. Set aside for 10 minutes.

Put 2 tablespoons of the reserved oil in the frying pan and heat
until smoking. Pour in the potato and egg mixture, spreading the
potatoes evenly in the pan. Cook for 1 minute, then reduce the
heat to medium and shake the pan often to stop it sticking.
When the eggs are brown underneath and top nearly firm, put
a large plate on the top and flip the omelette onto the plate.
Add 4 tablespoons of the remaining oil to the pan and slide the
omelette back into the pan to brown the other side. Lower the
heat and flip the omelette 3 more times, cooking 1 minute each
side, to give it a good shape. It should remain juicy inside.

Transfer to a plate, brush the top with oil and let stand until cool.
Serve in squares or wedges.

patatas bravas
potatoes in tomato sauce

3 tablespoons olive oil

600 g potatoes, cut into 2-cm cubes

1 small onion, grated

3 garlic cloves, crushed

2 tablespoons fino sherry

125 g canned chopped tomatoes

½ teaspoon dried chilli flakes, well crushed

½ teaspoon grated orange zest

1 teaspoon sugar

1 tablespoon freshly chopped flat leaf parsley

1 fresh bay leaf

serves 4

Heat 2 tablespoons of the olive oil in a frying pan, add the potatoes and mix well. Cook for 15 minutes until golden brown.

Meanwhile, heat the remaining oil in another frying pan, add the onion, and cook gently for 5 minutes. Add the garlic and sherry, then simmer for 1 minute to burn off the alcohol. Reduce the heat and add the tomatoes, chilli flakes, orange zest, sugar, parsley and bay leaf. Cook for 10 minutes, adding a little water to stop the mixture thickening too much.

Transfer the cooked potatoes to a serving bowl, pour over the tomato sauce and mix well. This can be made a day in advance and reheated before serving.

champiñones rellenos
stuffed mushrooms

Clean the mushrooms and remove the stems. Finely chop 2 of the stems and put them in a bowl. Add the milk and breadcrumbs and let soak for 10 minutes.

Add the onion, garlic, parsley, minced pork and ham. Mix together well, then cover with clingfilm and let marinate in the refrigerator overnight.

When ready to cook, put 1 heaped teaspoon of the mixture in each of the mushroom caps. Swirl over a little olive oil, then cook in a preheated oven at 180°C (350°F) Gas 4 for 15 minutes.

Remove from the oven, add a little pimiento to each one and sprinkle with lemon juice. Serve warm.

8 medium mushrooms

2 tablespoons milk

2 tablespoons breadcrumbs

2 tablespoons finely chopped onion

1 garlic clove, crushed

1 tablespoon freshly chopped flat leaf parsley

2 tablespoons minced pork

1 tablespoon finely chopped jamón serrano (Spanish ham)

1 tablespoon canned chopped pimiento

1 tablespoon freshly squeezed lemon juice

olive oil, for drizzling

serves 4

piquillos rellenos
spanish stuffed peppers

Drain the piquillo peppers, reserving the liquid. Pat dry with kitchen paper.

Heat the olive oil, garlic and part-drained white beans in a non-stick frying pan and mash with a fork to a thick, coarse purée. Add 1 tablespoon of the sherry vinegar and 1 tablespoon of bean liquid, stir, then season well with salt and pepper. Let cool slightly, then stuff each piquillo with the mixture and sprinkle with the thyme.

Cut each piquillo pepper into thick slices or leave whole. Serve on 4 plates, adding some salad greens to each. Trickle over a tablespoon of the bean liquid and a few drops of vinegar, if using, before serving.

Variation Instead of canned piquillos or pimientos, use 4 sweet red peppers, halved lengthways and deseeded. Grill them skin side up until blistered and black. Transfer to a plastic bag, seal and let steam. Rub off the skins, stuff with the mixture, roll up, then serve as in the main recipe.

185 g canned peeled piquillo peppers or pimientos

4 tablespoons olive oil

3–4 garlic cloves, chopped

550 g canned white beans, such as cannellini or butter beans, part-drained, liquid reserved

2 tablespoons sherry vinegar (optional)

a handful of fresh thyme or mint, chopped

a handful of baby salad greens such as spinach, watercress or flat leaf parsley

sea salt and freshly ground black pepper

serves 4

1 large aubergine,
about 350 g

150–200 g strong, meltable
cheese such as Cabrales or
Cheddar

100 g plain flour, seasoned
with salt and pepper

2 eggs, well beaten

about 500 ml olive,
sunflower or grapeseed
oil, for frying

salsa

250 g ripe red tomatoes,
chopped

4 tablespoons chilli oil
or olive oil mixed with
½ teaspoon Tabasco sauce

4 teaspoons red wine
vinegar or sherry vinegar

12 fresh basil leaves

sea salt and freshly ground
black pepper

cocktail sticks

an electric deep-fryer
(optional)

serves 4

berenjenas con queso
aubergine cheese fritters

Using a sharp, serrated knife, cut the aubergine crossways into
18–24 thin slices about 5 mm thick. Slice the cheese into pieces
of the same thickness. Cut and piece them together to fit,
sandwiching a piece of cheese between 2 pieces of aubergine.
To keep the 'sandwiches' closed during cooking, push a cocktail
stick, at an angle, through each one.

Put the seasoned flour on a plate. Pour the beaten egg into a
shallow dish. Dip the aubergine 'sandwiches' first into the flour,
then into the egg, then in flour again to coat well all over.

Fill a deep frying pan or an electric deep-fryer one-third full with
the oil, or to the manufacturer's recommended level. Heat to
190°C (375°F) or until a 1-cm cube of bread browns in 30
seconds. Slide some of the prepared 'sandwiches' into the hot oil
in batches of 3 and fry for 2–3 minutes on the first side. Using
tongs, turn and cook for 1–2 minutes on the other side or until
golden and crispy, with the cheese melting inside. Drain on
crumpled kitchen paper while you coat and cook the rest.

To make the salsa, put the tomatoes, chilli oil, vinegar, basil, salt
and pepper in a food processor. Pulse in brief bursts to a coarse
mixture, then serve with the fritters.

2 tablespoons olive oil

50 g jamón serrano (Spanish ham), finely chopped

½ onion, finely chopped

4 garlic cloves, crushed

1 courgette, chopped

2 tomatoes, skinned, deseeded and chopped

½ red pepper, deseeded and chopped

1 tablespoon chopped fresh oregano leaves

a pinch of oak-smoked sweet Spanish paprika (page 23)

sea salt and freshly ground white pepper

serves 4

pisto manchego
courgette, tomato and pepper stew

Heat the olive oil in a frying pan, add the ham and onion and cook over low heat for 5 minutes. Add the garlic, courgette, tomatoes, red pepper, oregano and paprika. Simmer over low heat for 15 minutes, then add salt and pepper to taste, and serve.

Note This is a popular vegetable dish from central Spain, where there are two versions – one with meat and one without. Simply leave the jamón serrano out for a vegetarian dish. Both versions can be made a day in advance and reheat well.

pimientos picantes
marinated peppers

Grill the peppers slowly until the skins are blistered and black.
Transfer to a plastic bag, seal and let steam. When cool, pull off
the skins and remove the seeds and membranes. Put the peppers
in a sieve set over a bowl to catch the juices, then cut into
1-cm strips.

Heat a heavy-based frying pan, then add the olive oil, vinegar,
thyme, rosemary, garlic, cayenne and the pepper juices. Cook
over low heat for 2 minutes. Add the peppers, capers, parsley
and salt and pepper to taste. Cook, stirring, for 1 minute. Remove
from the heat and let cool. Cover and chill overnight.

To serve, return to room temperature and serve on a thin slice of
bread. This dish can be kept in the refrigerator for up to a week.

3 small red peppers

3 tablespoons olive oil

50 ml sherry vinegar

a sprig of thyme

a sprig of rosemary

2 garlic cloves, sliced

½ teaspoon cayenne

1 tablespoon salted capers,
rinsed and drained

1 tablespoon freshly
chopped flat leaf parsley

sea salt and freshly ground
white pepper

thinly sliced bread,
to serve

serves 4

espinacas con piñones y pasas
spinach, pine nuts and raisins

Soak the raisins in warm water for 3 minutes, then drain.

Heat the olive oil in a frying pan, add the pine nuts and garlic, cook for 1 minute, then add the sherry and boil for 1 minute.

Add the spinach and paprika and toss well to coat with the juices. Cook over low heat for 5 minutes. Add the drained raisins and season with salt and pepper to taste, then serve.

50 g raisins

2 tablespoons fruity olive oil

25 g pine nuts, toasted in a dry frying pan

2 garlic cloves, sliced

3 tablespoons dry sherry

200 g spinach

a pinch of oak-smoked sweet Spanish paprika (page 23)

sea salt and freshly ground black pepper

serves 4

pinchos

2 tablespoons olive oil

1 garlic clove, crushed

½ teaspoon chilli flakes

leaves from 2 sprigs of thyme, plus extra to serve

100 g white asparagus, in can or jar*

2 tablespoons ground almonds

½ canned pimiento, chopped

8 slices of white bread, lightly toasted

sea salt and freshly ground black pepper

serves 4

Put the olive oil, garlic, chilli flakes and thyme in a saucepan, bring to the boil, then remove from the heat. Let cool.

Put the asparagus in a blender and pulse until smooth. Slowly add the strained oil and blend again. Mix in the ground almonds and salt and pepper to taste.

Slice the pimiento into thin strips. Spoon the asparagus mixture onto the toasted bread and top with the sliced pimiento. Add a few thyme leaves and serve on a tray for your guests to help themselves.

*Note White asparagus, sold in cans or jars, is a traditional Spanish ingredient.

queso frito
fried cheese

Cut all the rind off the Manchego cheese and cut the cheese into 1-cm wedges.

Put the flour on a small plate and, working in batches of 6, dip each wedge in the flour, then in the beaten egg, then in the breadcrumbs.

Heat half the olive oil in a non-stick frying pan over medium heat, then fry the wedges in batches until golden – about 45 seconds each side. Drain on kitchen paper.

Wipe out the pan (to get rid of burnt breadcrumbs) and fry the remaining batches in the same way.

Sprinkle with a pinch of paprika, if liked, and serve with quince paste and olives, if using.

*Note Membrillo is a thick paste made from quinces, a golden fruit related to the apple and pear, available in autumn. Quinces are cooked into puddings, jellies or jams, and into this sweetly smoky paste. Membrillo is also served with a good Manchego cheese instead of dessert in Spain.

275–300 g semi-cured Manchego cheese, 3 months old

2 tablespoons plain flour

1 egg, beaten

150 g lightly dried fine fresh white breadcrumbs

150 ml olive oil

a pinch of oak-smoked sweet Spanish paprika (page 23)

membrillo (quince paste; optional)*

or mixed olives, to serve (optional)

serves 6

alioli

4–6 garlic cloves, crushed

1 whole egg

1 egg yolk

1 teaspoon freshly squeezed lemon juice

500 ml extra virgin olive oil

sea salt and freshly ground black pepper

serves 4

Put the garlic, egg and egg yolk and lemon juice in a food processor. Blend until pale yellow. Keep the motor running and slowly pour in the olive oil, a little at a time. Blend well, until thick and silky, then add salt and pepper to taste. Serve at room temperature with fish or meat.

Alioli with potatoes

Put 500 g unpeeled new potatoes in a saucepan, cover with cold water, add a pinch of salt and boil until tender. Drain and let cool. Slip off the skins, cut the potatoes into bite-sized pieces, then serve with alioli as a dip.

aceitunas en escabeche
marinated olives

Put the olives in a bowl, add the garlic, chillies, pepper, lemon, parsley, bay leaves and salt. Mix, then transfer to a jar into which they just fit, then pour over the vinegar and the reserved brine. Shake well and let marinate at room temperature for 2 weeks.

Variation To marinate green olives, add 2 extra garlic cloves to the marinade and replace the chillies and other ingredients with 1 tablespoon crushed coriander seeds, 1 tablespoon crushed fennel seeds, 6 thyme sprigs, 4 rosemary sprigs and the zest and juice of 1 orange. Cover with olive oil and marinate for 6 days.

500 g black Spanish olives, drained with brine reserved

4 garlic cloves, sliced

2 dried red chillies

8 black peppercorns

1 slice of lemon

4 sprigs of parsley

4 fresh bay leaves

a pinch of salt

300 ml red wine vinegar

almendras saladas
salted almonds

Pour 2 cm depth of olive oil into a saucepan and heat to 195°C (380°F). Test with a sugar thermometer, or drop in a small cube of bread – it should turn golden in about 30 seconds.

Fry the almonds until lightly golden. Drain, sprinkle with the salt and paprika and mix well. Let cool slightly before serving.

200 g blanched almonds

1 teaspoon coarse sea salt, finely ground

½ teaspoon oak-smoked sweet Spanish paprika (page 23)

olive oil, for frying

index

picture credits

Martin Brigdale
Pages 1, 6, 11, 14, 19, 28, 30, 35, 39, 44, 47, 56

David Munns
Page 2

Ian Wallace
Page 3

Peter Cassidy
Pages 5, 8, 12, 17, 20, 22, 25, 27, 33, 36, 41, 42, 49, 50, 52, 55, 59, 60

Noel Murphy
Endpapers

recipe credits

Julz Beresford
Pages 9, 13, 16, 21, 23, 24, 26, 32, 37, 38, 40, 43, 48, 51, 53, 54, 58, 61

Clare Ferguson
Pages 15, 18, 29, 31, 45, 46

Linda Tubby
Pages 10, 34, 57